Everything You Need to Know About

STD
Sexually Transmitted Disease

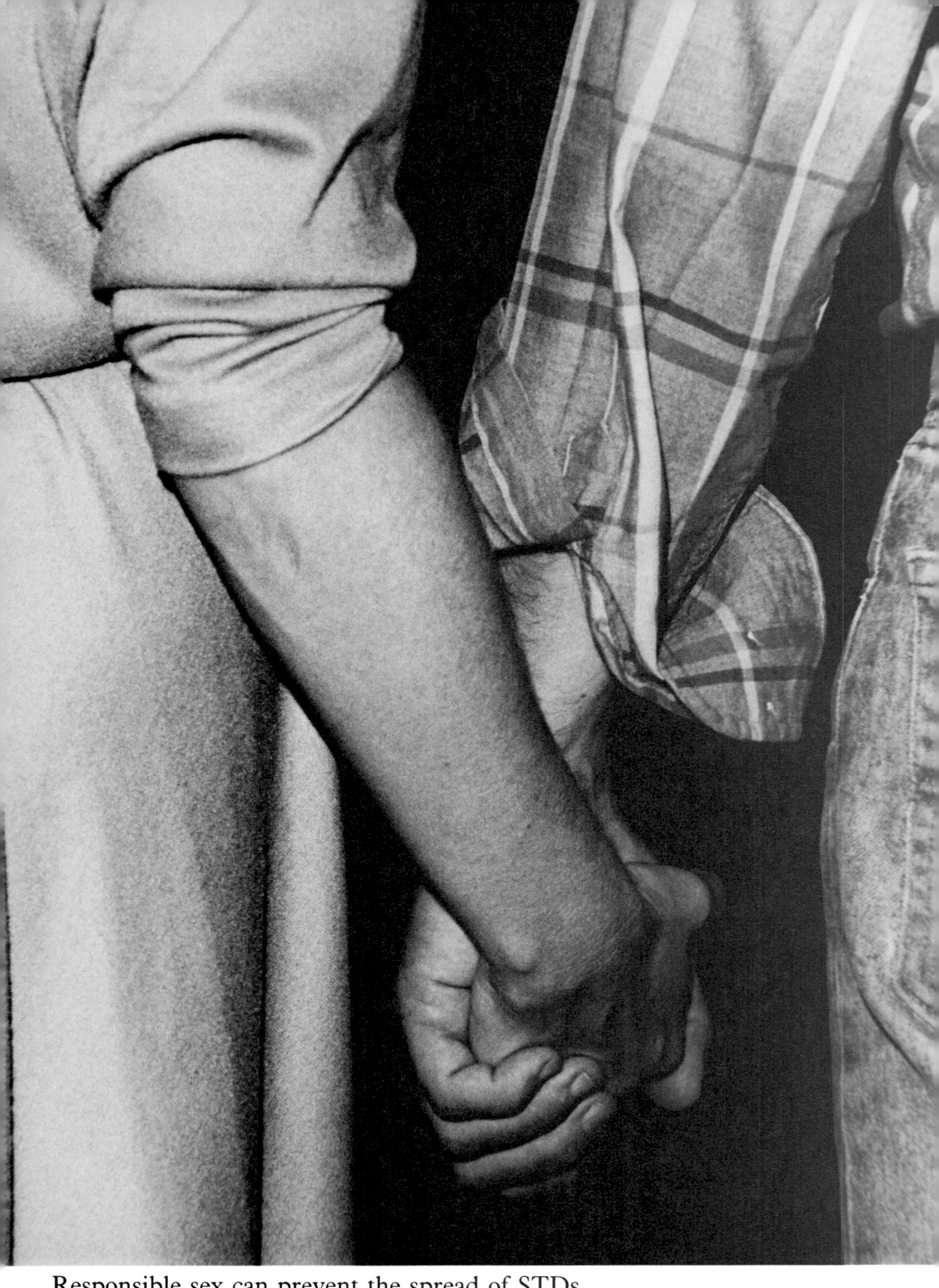

Responsible sex can prevent the spread of STDs.

• THE NEED TO KNOW LIBRARY •

Everything You Need to Know About

STD
Sexually Transmitted Disease

Samuel G. Woods

Laura Diskavich, M.S., R.N.C.
Technical Consultant

Series Editor: Evan Stark, Ph.D.

THE ROSEN PUBLISHING GROUP, INC.
NEW YORK

Published in 1990, 1994 by The Rosen Publishing Group, Inc.
29 East 21st Street, New York, NY 10010

Revised Edition 1994

Manufactured in the United States of America.

Library of Congress Cataloging-in-Publication Data

Woods, Samual G.
Everything you need to know about STD (sexually transmitted diseases) / Samual G. Woods.
(The Need to know library)
Includes bibliographical references.
Index.
Summary: Describes sexually transmitted diseases, including AIDS, syphilis, gonorrhea, and genital herpes, and discusses their medical dangers and where to get help.
ISBN 0-8239-1799-1
I. Title. II. Series.
RC200.W66 1989
616.95'1—dc20

89-70118
CIP
AC

Contents

Introduction

On November 7, 1991, basketball superstar Magic Johnson shocked the world. At a press conference, he announced that he was HIV-positive. At first no one could believe it. How could someone so rich, so famous, and so talented have a deadly virus—the AIDS virus?

Magic Johnson's decision to go public with the news about his condition was a very brave thing for him to do. He knew that telling the world his story would show people that *anyone* can get AIDS (acquired immunodeficiency syndrome). Even people who were idols to millions. Magic's story was a major breakthrough in AIDS prevention. Magic convinced millions of young adults how serious the AIDS epidemic really is. And it got them talking about ways to prevent AIDS, too.

AIDS is not the only common sexually transmitted disease. Syphilis, gonorrhea, herpes, genital warts, and chlamydia are also infecting hundreds of millions of people worldwide each year. AIDS is always in the news. But the other STDs are hardly ever talked about. If they are, it is more often in whispers than out loud.

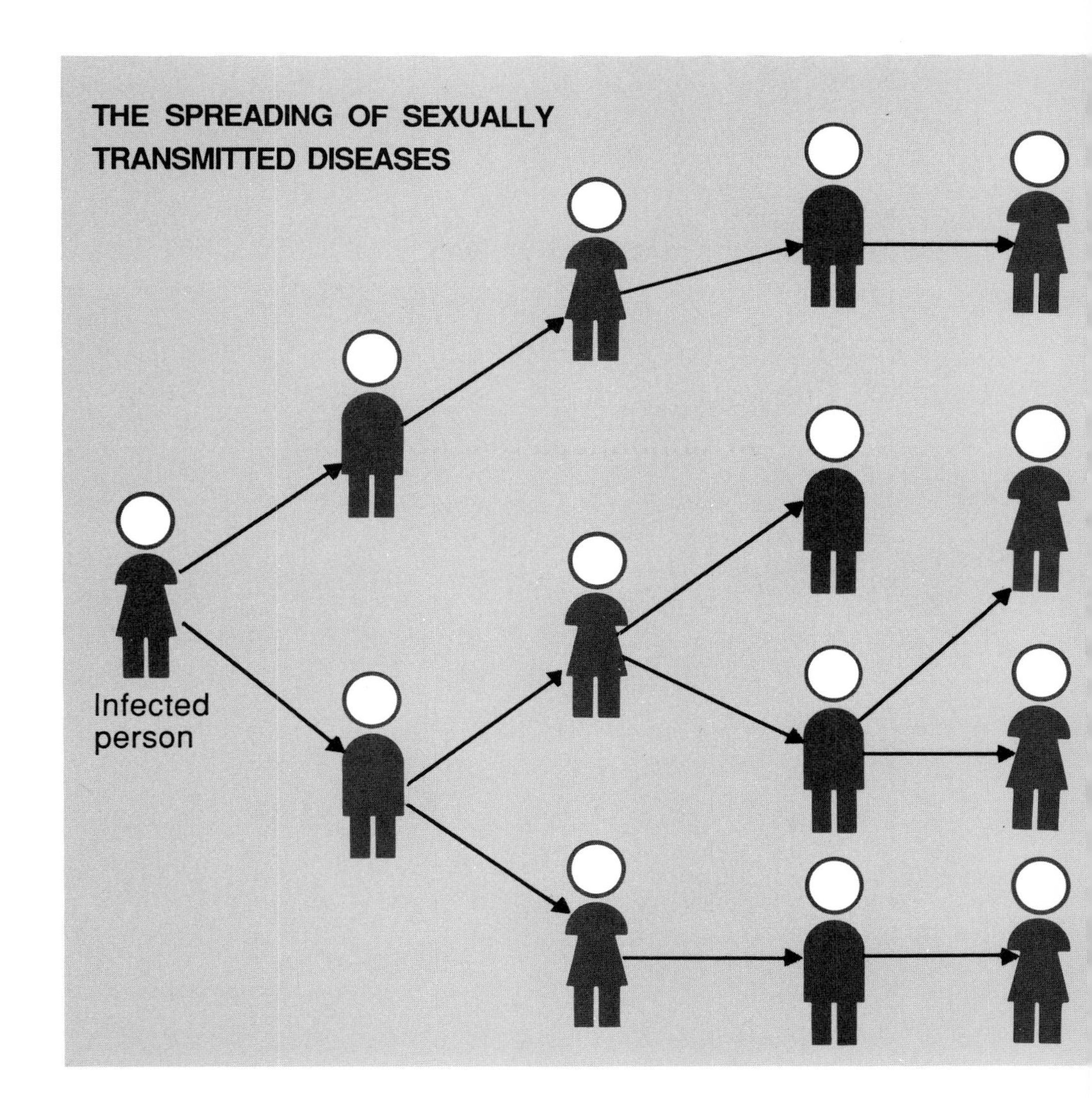

STDs have been around since the beginning of recorded time in almost every society and civilization. For many years, STDs were grouped together and called *venereal disease* (VD). Some of these diseases have almost disappeared. Others have become large-scale health threats. For a better understanding of all the diseases transmitted by sexual contact, they are now commonly referred to as STDs.

There are two major reasons why STDs are so hard to control. The first reason is how easily they spread. One person can be indirectly responsible for infecting hundreds—even thousands—of other people. That is because each person that becomes infected can, in turn, infect hundreds or thousands of others. And each of those thousands can infect thousands more.

The second reason why STDs are hard to control is because people are often too embarrassed to talk about them. Talking about sex makes most people uncomfortable. That is why talk about responsible sex is often avoided. But it is important that people—sexually active or not— learn the facts. When people know the facts about STDs, they are much less likely to get infected.

Many people in society have also made others who suffer from STDs feel "dirty" or "bad" for being infected. If people feel ashamed, they are much less likely to talk about their problems. And they are much less likely to get treatment.

Most STDs are very dangerous. Some can cause death. Others can hurt a person for life. All of them threaten the health and well-being of others as well.

Today, people are more aware of STDs than ever before. The spread of AIDS has made people more concerned about "safer sex." But more sex education is still needed. There are millions of people who don't practice safer sex. Many of those people get STDs because they don't know the facts about sexual contact and the risks involved. They don't know what the common symptoms of STDs are. And they don't know how most of these diseases can be easily prevented.

This book will tell you the facts about sexually transmitted diseases. It will talk about sex and how your body works. It will discuss safer sex and will tell you what to consider if and when you decide to have sex. It will talk about recognizing the early signs of an STD and how to get treatment. And it will talk about the best ways to prevent these diseases in the first place.

Most important, this book will show you that there is no reason to be embarrassed about STDs. These diseases are very common. All of them can be prevented. And most can be cured. The most dangerous practice of all, you'll realize, is never learning about them in the first place.

Getting the facts about health risks is important.

Chapter 1

Facts about Sexually Transmitted Diseases

It is estimated that more than 70 million people in the United States alone are infected with some form of sexually transmitted disease. Though worldwide data is incomplete, some experts guess that anywhere from 200 to 400 million people around the globe suffer from STDs. Sexually transmitted diseases are a big problem. A problem that is growing every day.

Though each STD is unique, all STDs share certain similarities. They are all transmitted through sex or intimate body contact. And they are all dangerous if they are not treated. Some can cause slow and painful death.

Many STDs have similar symptoms. But some have no symptoms at all. This is especially true for women. Common symptoms may include discharge from the penis or vagina; redness or itching of the genitals; pain or burning during sex or during urination; sores, blisters, or bumps in the genital area. One thing is exactly the same for all STDs: They must all be treated as soon as possible.

What Is a Disease?

A disease is something that makes a person sick. When a person is sick, the body changes. This makes the person feel ill. Sometimes many parts of the body stop working as they should. This can cause death.

Diseases can be caused by different kinds of germs. A germ is a *microscopic* invader in the body. It is so small that you need a special instrument called a microscope to see it. Germs get into the body in many different ways. And when they are inside the body, they can cause trouble.

Germs come in many different forms. Some germs are bacteria. Bacteria are found almost everywhere. Many bacteria do not harm humans. There are bacteria in the air we breathe and the water we drink. There are even bacteria in our bodies. Some bacteria cause disease in humans. Food poisoning, for example, is caused by bacteria.

Other germs are fungi and parasites. Fungi are plant-like organisms. A mushroom is a fungus.

Some fungi are very tiny. Some of the tiny fungi can cause disease and irritation to humans. Athlete's foot is caused by a fungus. Human parasites are tiny animals that attach themselves to the human body. They use the human body as "food." They live off the materials in the body. Some parasites can be seen easily by the naked eye. Crabs (pubic lice) are a parasite.

Viruses are also a kind of germ. A virus is something that gets into the cells of the body. The cells are among the smallest parts of a human body. All our body parts are made up of billions of cells. A virus attacks the cells and makes them act differently. They cannot perform their normal jobs.

A cold is caused by a virus. The "flu" (short for influenza) is also a virus. When you get sick with these diseases you have a virus inside you. You begin to feel ill because your body is suffering from the invasion by the virus. The symptoms you get—cough, fever, and aches—are all because of the invading virus that is attacking your cells.

Many of the diseases we will talk about are caused by bacteria and viruses.

Sexually transmitted diseases are called *contagious* diseases. Contagious means you can catch something from another person. They are sexually transmitted diseases because you catch them by having sexual contact with another person who has the disease. This touching could involve the penis, the vagina, the rectum, or the mouth.

Contagious diseases are serious and scary. They can spread very fast. One person can spread the disease to hundreds or thousands of other people. Here's an example: One infected person has sex with ten people. Then each of those people has sex with ten other people. That means that 101 people have been exposed to the disease. What if each of those people has sex with ten people? Then 1,110 people will be exposed. And all because of *one* infected person.

How Can STDs Be Prevented?

When and if you decide to have sex, the best way to prevent STDs is to follow responsible sexual behavior. This is commonly referred to as "safer sex." Safer sex generally means using condoms. Condoms are rubber casings that slip over the erect penis before sex. They prevent direct genital contact between partners. Without direct genital contact, the chance of giving someone a disease is much smaller. Condoms are also a very effective form of birth control. Other birth control items, such as diaphragms, foam, and suppositories, can protect females partially from STDs. They can also protect males from certain diseases. Contraceptive jelly and "the pill" do not prevent STDs.

Safer sex also means knowing about your partner's past sexual behavior. This is important because the people your partner has had sex with can have an effect on your health.

Are STDs Getting Worse?

Infections of some STDs have gone down in the last 20 years. But other STDs have been discovered. All in all, more people in the 1990s are getting some kind of STD than ever before.

It is estimated that each year more than 7 million people in North America are infected with some kind of STD. Teens make up a large part of that number. More than 2,000 teens get syphilis or gonorrhea every day. Thousands of teens each month discover they are infected with the AIDS virus. About half of all the people in America who have STDs are 25 years old or younger.

Although the total number of people with STDs has been rising in recent years, many people are learning prevention. As more and more people learn the facts about preventing STDs, the growth rate of infection will slow down.

STDs: Facts at a Glance

1. STDs are highly infectious. Many have similar symptoms. They spread by sexual contact and can affect the penis, vagina, rectum, anus, and other organs.
2. STDs are very dangerous if left untreated.
3. Most STDs can be cured if treated early. AIDS and herpes cannot be cured.
4. "Safer sex" greatly reduces the chances of transmitting an STD. Safer sex means using a condom *every* time you have sex.

Chapter 2

Some Facts about the Human Body

STDs are transmitted through sexual contact. It is important to know how the human sex organs work. Often it is the sexual organs that show signs of an STD.

Different parts of the body are called organs. Every organ in the body is made up of tissue. And all tissue is made up of millions of cells. Cells, as we learned, are parts of the body that can be infected by different kinds of germs.

The Male Sex Organs

Some male sex organs are outside the body and some are inside. Outside are the penis and the testicles (or testes). The testes are in a sac called

FEMALE REPRODUCTIVE SYSTEM

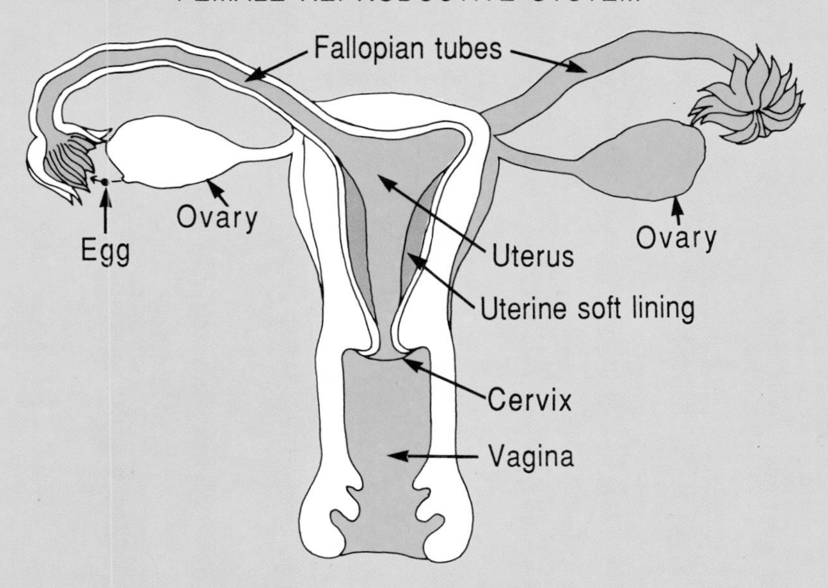

MALE REPRODUCTIVE SYSTEM

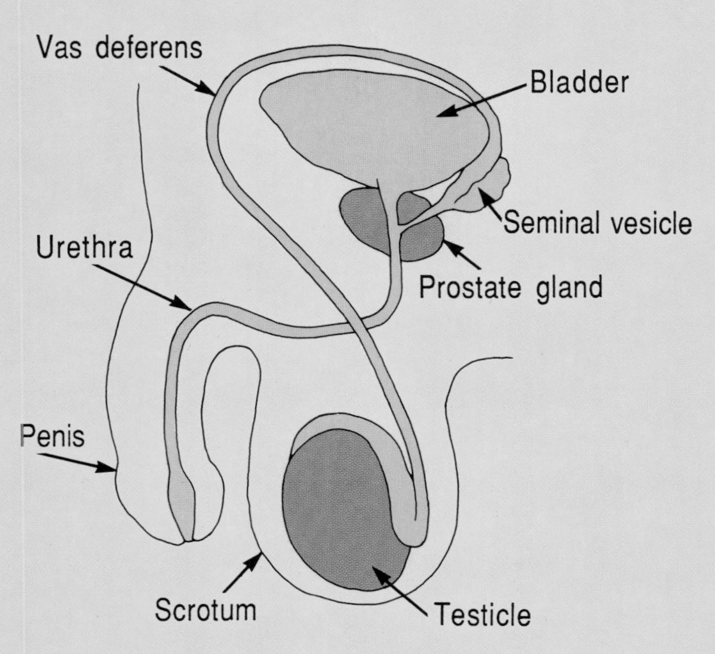

the scrotum. The testes produce sperm. Sperm are in semen (see-men), the male fertilizing liquid.

Males with an STD usually pass the disease through the penis. In most cases, the bacteria are present in a tube inside the penis. The male may not even be aware of the presence of any bacteria. He may function quite normally. When the erect penis is stimulated, it releases the semen in a series of muscular spasms called ejaculation. The bacteria are passed through the penis with the fluid that contains the sperm.

The Female Sex Organs

The external female sex organ is the clitoris. The clitoris becomes stimulated during sexual activity. The clitoris is located in front of the vagina. The vagina is the passage that leads to the uterus (womb). The fallopian tubes come out from either side of the uterus. An ovary is at the end of each tube. About each month one of the ovaries produces a mature egg cell. The egg then bursts out of the ovary and into a fallopian tube. When the egg is in the tube, it may be fertilized (impregnated) by a sperm. If the egg is fertilized by a sperm, it will attach itself to the wall of the uterus and begin to grow. It will become an embryo. Then it will become a fetus. Finally, it will be ready to be born as a baby. If it is not fertilized, the egg will be flushed out of the body through menstruation (the menstrual "period").

The Effects of Sexual Intercourse

During sex there is usually an exchange of bodily fluids. The transmission involves a penis and a vagina, or a rectum, or a mouth. As we have heard, an infected person can pass a sexually transmitted germ to a partner. The germ can be passed through close bodily contact or exchange of bodily fluids. Kissing also exchanges a bodily fluid, saliva. But kissing is not usually very dangerous. Kissing may be dangerous if one person has an STD infection in the mouth or throat.

Ways to Reduce the Risks

Make it a habit to use condoms. Using condoms is smart. Condoms perform two very important jobs. They greatly reduce the chance of giving someone a sexually transmitted disease. And they greatly reduce the chance of pregnancy.

Some people do not want to "bother" with using condoms. A condom must be put on an erect penis, one that is stimulated. For some people this means "stopping at a bad time." Many people do not want to interrupt their lovemaking in order to put on a condom. Many people are probably embarrassed by it, too. And some people are afraid that their partner will lose interest in lovemaking if they stop even briefly. But a condom may keep you from getting AIDS, or getting another disease. And it may prevent pregnancy. PREVENTION IS WORTH A TINY INTERRUPTION!

Many people don't know that they have a sexually transmitted disease. They may infect several sexual partners.

ONE WAY
WALK

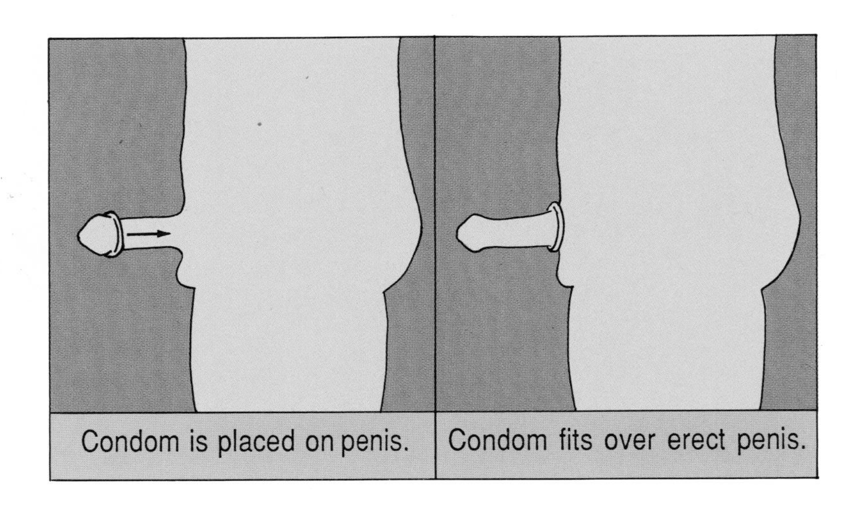

Condom is placed on penis. Condom fits over erect penis.

Condoms can be bought in many places. Since AIDS has become a serious worry, condoms are more widely available. In addition to being sold in any drugstore, condoms can often be found at school health clinics, Planned Parenthood offices, your doctor's office, at gas stations, and in public rest rooms.

Important note: Never use a condom from an open wrapper. And never use a condom more than once. Be prepared to use a fresh, new condom each time you have sex.

Know about your partner. As we saw in Chapter 1, STDs can spread very easily. Sex with someone who has had sex with many other people in a short period of time is a risk. Each person that your partner has had sex with increases the chances that he or she has a disease. And that increases your chances of getting it.

Be aware of your body. Look carefully at your body. Know what your body looks like normally. Pay attention to how you feel as well as how you look. Keep an eye out for any changes in your body. Pay attention to these changes. Ask yourself how long they have been there. Are they going away or are they getting worse? Could these changes be caused by something else or could they be signs of an STD?

Be aware of your partner's body. Watch for any changes in appearance or any other problems you may see.

STDs and the Body: Facts at a Glance

1. Male sex organs are the penis, the testes, and the scrotum.
2. Female sex organs are the clitoris and the vagina.
3. STDs are transmitted when bodily fluids are exchanged during close body contact or sex.
4. There are many effective ways to reduce the risks of getting an STD. One of the best ways is to use a condom if you are involved in sexual activity.

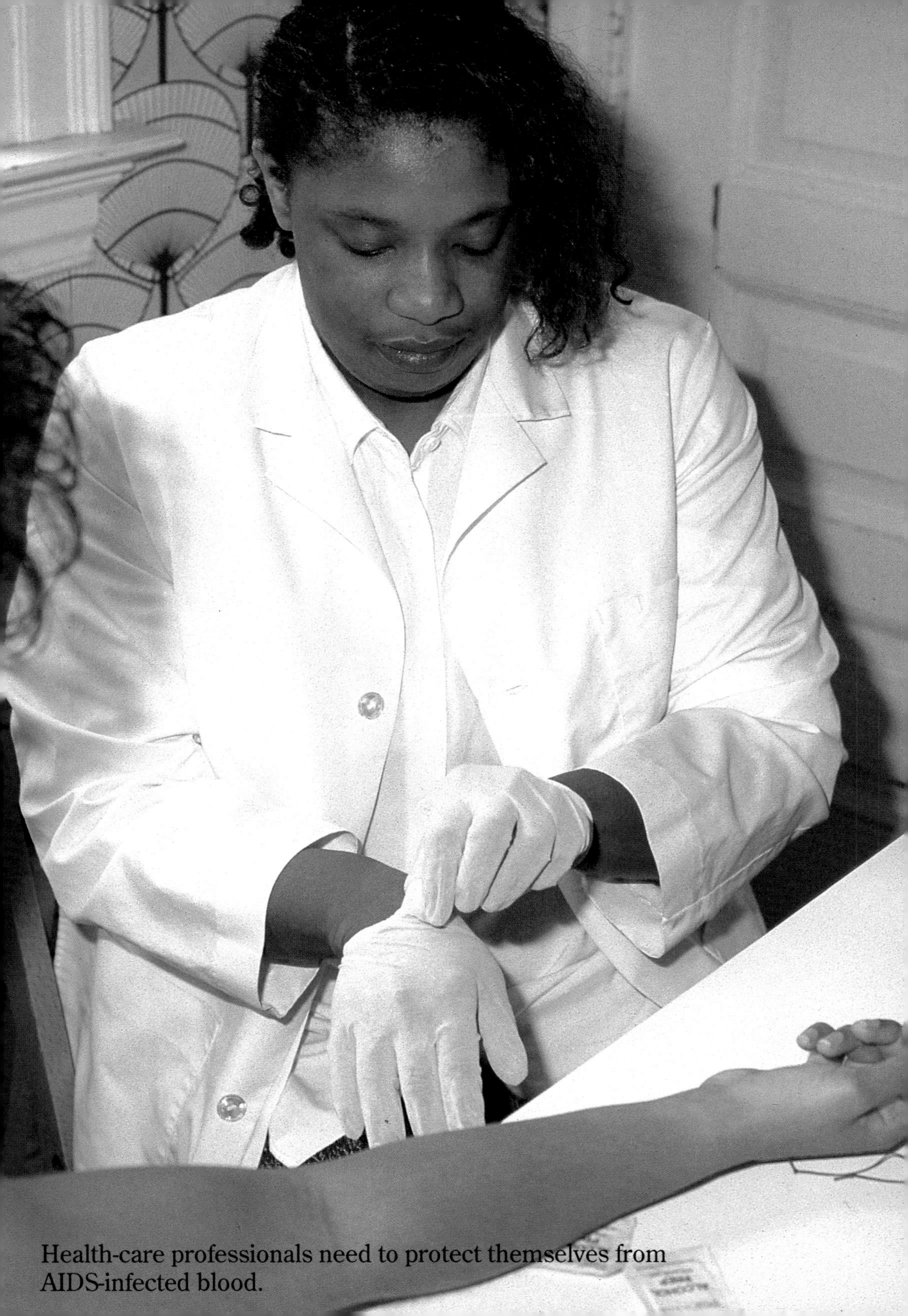

Health-care professionals need to protect themselves from AIDS-infected blood.

Chapter 3

AIDS: The Modern Epidemic

AIDS has become one of the most talked about and most alarming subjects in the world today. It is constantly in the news. It has become a key issue in politics. It has claimed the lives of some of the world's best-known and most beloved figures. AIDS is by far the most dangerous disease of our time.

Before 1980, there were less than a handful of reported AIDS cases. Even then, few doctors knew what AIDS really was. By 1983, about 4,500 cases had been diagnosed and 2,000 people had died from the virus. Only five years later, more than 100,000 people had been diagnosed and 60,000 had died. Less than five years after that, by 1992, the number of diagnoses had more than doubled and over 153,000 people were dead from AIDS.

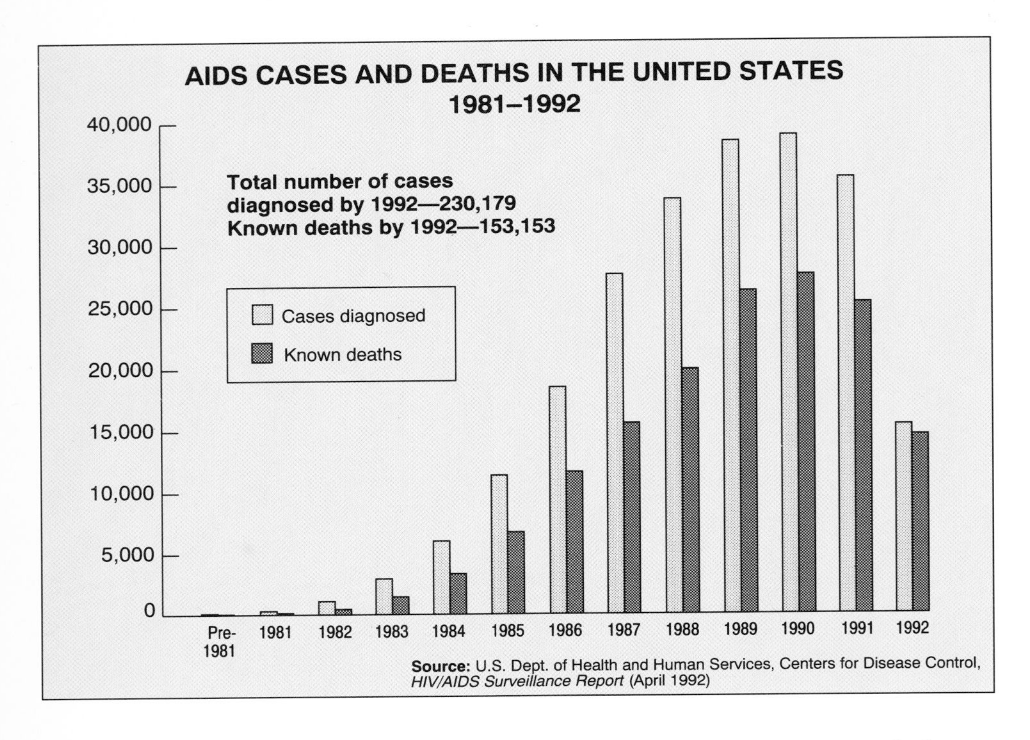

The Centers for Disease Control estimated that diagnosed AIDS cases would rise to about 500,000 by the end of 1993. It also estimated that, all together, more than 1 million people in the United States may be infected with the HIV virus.

AIDS has become a national priority in many countries, including the United States, Canada, and Great Britain. Billions of dollars have already been spent in search of a cure and a vaccine. Researchers know much more about AIDS today than they did 10 years ago. They know how AIDS is transmitted and how it affects the body. They even have some medicines that seem to be effective in helping to control the disease. But a cure for AIDS has still not been found.

What Is AIDS?

AIDS stands for acquired immunodeficiency syndrome. That's a medical way of saying that the AIDS virus (HIV) attacks the body's immune system. The immune system is the body's system for fighting disease and infection.

When an invading virus or germ enters the body, the immune system immediately begins to fight it. White blood cells try to kill the cells that have been invaded by the virus. They try to stop them from multiplying. If the white blood cells cannot kill enough of the virus cells, the virus will take over. The person will be sick.

The AIDS virus almost always enters the body through bodily fluids that are shared between two people. This can happen when an infected person shares a needle with a person who is not infected. Or it can happen when an infected person has sex with a person who is not infected. During sex, the AIDS virus is transported in the semen (sperm-carrying fluid) of the male. The semen transmits the virus into the body of the partner by way of the vagina, the rectum, or the mouth.

Once the virus is inside, it begins to grow and multiply. Then it attacks the immune system. Doctors do not know everything about how the immune system is destroyed. And they do not know how to stop the AIDS virus from multiplying. They do know, however, that once the virus has started to do its work, the body will soon lose its ability to fight disease. Once the immune system is destroyed, the victim cannot fight off even the most common viruses and germs. It is only a matter of time until the victim's body cannot function. Then the person will die.

What Are the Symptoms?

Often, the symptoms of AIDS take a while to appear. People can be carrying the virus for a number of years and still appear to be healthy. This period is called the "incubation period." It is the time when the virus is "growing" inside the body. All STDs have an incubation period.

There are many symptoms of AIDS. Patients may have some or all of the symptoms. Each body's immune system will resist AIDS in a different way. The most common symptoms of AIDS are:

- extreme weakness and fatigue
- swollen lymph glands
- rapid weight loss
- stubborn cough
- coated tongue and throat
- easy bruising and unexplained bleeding
- frequent fever
- night sweats
- bumps, rashes, tumors, or other strange developments on the skin
- trouble recovering from common illness, such as cold or flu

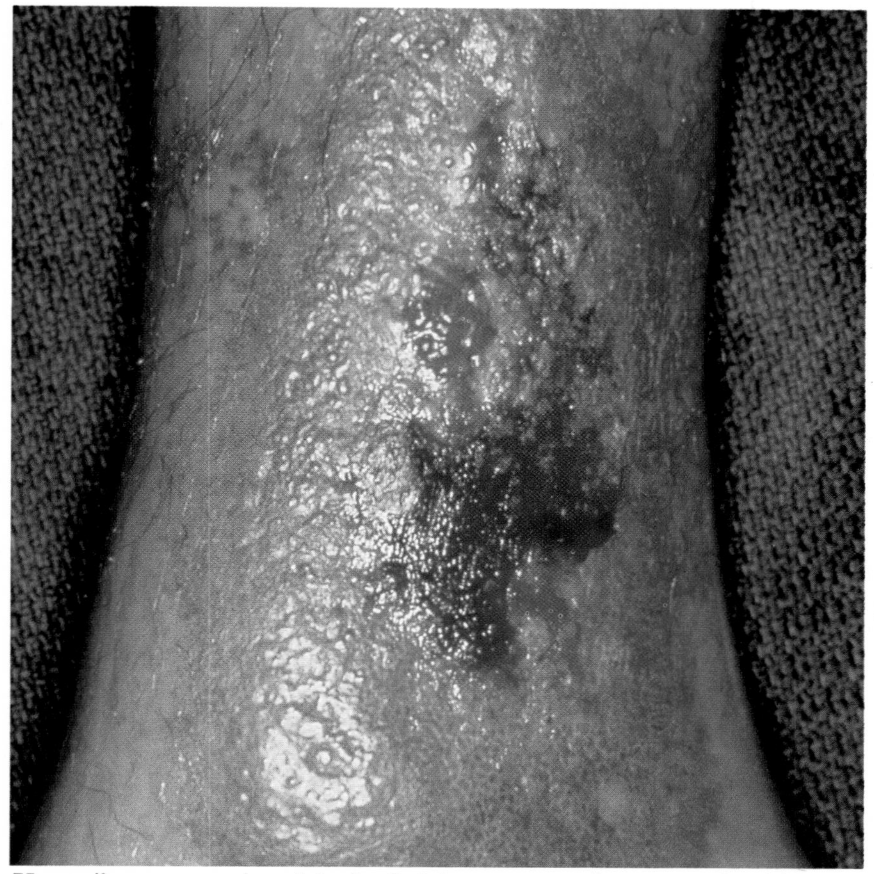

Kaposi's sarcoma is a kind of skin cancer often seen in AIDS patients.

Can Anyone Get AIDS?

Not long ago, most people thought AIDS was just a disease that endangered homosexuals and drug abusers. But then other stories began to be told. A child in elementary school was found to have the HIV virus. A female college student became infected. The world lost ballet great Rudolf Nuryev and tennis legend Arthur Ashe to the disease as well.

All these stories, and the many others in the news every day, have proven that anyone can get AIDS. Some people, however, are at greater risk than others.

In the United States, homosexual males make up about 58% of all adult and teenage AIDS cases. Drug users that use dirty (infected) needles make up another 23% of the total. These figures indicate that 19% of all AIDS cases are found in other populations. If the Centers for Disease Control estimates are correct, that would mean more than 190,000 lower-risk people have become infected.

About 6% of all reported U.S. AIDS cases are among heterosexuals. This may seem like a low percentage. But disease experts say that AIDS is spreading faster through heterosexual populations than any other group. Those at the highest risk are people who have multiple sex partners and those with other STDs. A 1992 report showed that 19% of American high school students have had sex with four or more people. This kind of sexual activity puts teenagers at high risk for AIDS.

Not everyone who gets AIDS has had sex with an infected person or used drugs. Babies born to mothers with AIDS have a 50% chance of carrying the virus. People who had blood transfusions before 1985 also run a small risk. Before 1985, blood in hospitals and clinics was not prescreened for AIDS. Arthur Ashe became infected from blood he got during an operation before 1985.

Prevention and Cure

No cure has yet been developed for AIDS. Researchers are testing a number of vaccines that may prevent infection, but no results are final. Many drugs that combat the virus are also being tested. Though some have promise, only a drug called AZT has been shown to actually prolong the life of an AIDS patient.

Because there is no cure for AIDS, prevention is of utmost importance. Not having sex is one way to greatly reduce the risk of AIDS. Not using illegal drugs and needles is another way. If you decide to have sex, the best protection against AIDS and other STDs is the condom. In addition, you should find out as much about your partner's sexual history as you can. Once you have sex, your partner's history becomes yours as well.

AIDS: Facts at a Glance

1. HIV is not AIDS. HIV is the virus that causes AIDS. Experts believe more than 1 million people in the United States alone may be infected with HIV.
2. The AIDS virus attacks the body's immune system. It is transmitted through blood or semen.
3. AIDS is fatal. There is no cure.
4. The risk of getting AIDS is greatly reduced by using condoms and practicing "safer sex."

Sores on the lip might be a sign of a venereal disease.

Chapter 4

Syphilis: The Well-Disguised Danger

Syphilis is caused by a tiny germ called a *spiro-chete* (spy-ro-keet). Spirochetes are bacteria. They are very, very small and can live almost anywhere in the body.

Syphilis is also contagious (catching). That means one person gets it from another person who has it. Syphilis is a venereal disease. It is transmitted only through sexual contact.

Syphilis has a rather long incubation period. That means it takes a long time for it to grow and be seen. The incubation period for syphilis is three weeks to three months.

After incubation, a sore appears at the infected area. The sore is infectious for as long as it can be seen. The spirochetes are in the sore. The spirochetes carry the disease.

A syphilis sore is called a chancre (shan-ker). A chancre can look like a cut or a rash. A person can become infected with syphilis by having direct contact with an open sore. The sore may be in the mouth, vagina, rectum, or on the penis of an infected person. This contact happens during sex with an infected person. During sex, the man's penis comes in contact with the vagina, rectum, or mouth of his partner. These are usually the organs that have the syphilis sores. And that is when the spirochetes (germs) move into the body of the healthy person.

Dear Joan,

I'm sorry I haven't written in a while. I was a little upset last week. Something happened that has never happened to me before. I noticed a red sore on my lower lip. It didn't hurt but it looked terrible.

Of course, I told Ted right away. And we stopped having sex right away. I went to the doctor immediately. She said it looked like syphilis. I had a test done. It was syphilis. I got very worried. But the doctor told me that it would be cured in a very short time. All I needed was some medicine called penicillin. The doctor also said it was very good that I came right away. Evidently, it is best to treat these things as soon as possible.

Ted also went to his doctor. He had syphilis, too. Anyway, we're both feeling fine now. And I look forward to seeing you next weekend.

Karen

The Stages of Syphilis

A chancre sore will develop on the part of the body where the infection was passed. This is called the *primary lesion of syphilis.* Usually this sore will look terrible. It may look red and it may be wet. But this sore does not usually cause pain. It is just very unsightly.

Sometimes the primary sore will be easy to see. It may be on the penis. But many syphilis sores are not easy to see. They can be inside the vagina, or under the foreskin of the penis. They can also be under the tongue or inside the rectum. Often, the infected person doesn't see the sore.

After a few weeks the chancre disappears. When a chancre heals, there is a feeling of relief. Often the infected person feels as if the syphilis has "gone away." But it has not gone away. It is just "hiding" inside the body until later.

If the sore has disappeared and the syphilis is still not treated, the disease gets more serious. It enters the *secondary stage.* The secondary stage is anywhere from six weeks to six months after the infection began.

In the secondary stage, the spirochetes have multiplied throughout the whole body. The symptoms can take different forms. Most symptoms are in the mucous membranes and the skin. The mucous membranes are the soft linings inside the body cavities, like the nose and mouth. A rash can now break out on the skin. It can be anywhere on the body. It is often on the palms of the hands and the soles of the feet. Patches of hair can fall out, too.

When these symptoms appear, it means the person is very contagious. A partner will get syphilis from the person. The symptoms can last for weeks. Eventually they go away. But even when they go away, the syphilis stays.

Latent Syphilis

After the second stage disappears, the person has *latent syphilis.* Latent means hidden. A person with latent syphilis may no longer have any symptoms. But a blood test would still show the disease.

Most people are not infectious after they have had syphilis for one year. They will no longer pass the disease to others. But if syphilis is not treated for a long time it will cause more serious damage. Untreated patients can develop brain damage. The spirochetes will destroy the tissues in the brain. This often causes insanity that cannot be cured.

There are other symptoms of untreated syphilis. Spinal cord damage and paralysis can occur. Many victims lose their ability to walk and also to see. These are all results of the spirochetes slowly damaging the tissues of organs.

Syphilis and Pregnancy

It is very dangerous for a pregnant woman to have syphilis. A pregnant woman with syphilis will pass the disease to her child. Syphilis in newborn infants can cause deformities and even death.

How Is Syphilis Treated?

Treatment for syphilis is simple. That is so especially if the disease is treated early.

Syphilis can be treated and cured by penicillin. If a patient is allergic to penicillin, another antibiotic can be prescribed by a doctor.

Syphilis in the 1990s

The reported number of syphilis cases in the world has gone down considerably since the 1970s. But syphilis is still a major health threat. In the United States alone, there were an estimated 43,000 cases of syphilis in 1991. The World Health Organization estimates that 3.5 million people worldwide have infectious syphilis.

Syphilis: Facts at a Glance

1. Syphilis is transmitted through sexual contact. The disease is caused by bacteria called spirochetes.
2. There are three stages of syphilis. First is the primary stage. Then there is a secondary stage. Finally, syphilis becomes latent, or hidden.
3. Syphilis can be cured early on with penicillin or other medications.
4. Syphilis can cause serious physical damage if left untreated.

If one partner infects the other with an STD, both partners must be treated by a doctor.

Chapter 5

Gonorrhea and Chlamydia: Growing Problems

Gonorrhea and chlamydia are common STDs. Most people have heard of gonorrhea. But many people do not know about chlamydia. Chlamydia can cause serious problems if it is not treated.

Many people make a joke of gonorrhea. They refer to it by many other names. They call it "the clap," or "the drip." But gonorrhea is a serious disease. It should be treated as soon as possible.

Dear Danny,

I'm sorry I yelled at you last night. I know this whole thing isn't your fault. You had no idea that what you had was gonorrhea. I shouldn't have blamed you for "burning me."

It's both our faults, really. We should have used a condom all the time. I think that once or twice without a condom was enough to give the bacteria to me.

I think we should both go to the doctor's office together tomorrow. Will you come with me? That way we can get treated together.

Talk to you tonight.

Love,
Maria

What Causes Gonorrhea?

Gonorrhea is caused by the bacteria called *Neisseria gonorrhea.* These bacteria cannot live outside the body. They live in the mucous membranes. Those are the soft linings inside organs like the eyelids, the mouth, the rectum, the penis, or the vagina.

It is not true that you can get gonorrhea by casual contact. You cannot get it from a doorknob or a toilet seat. You can't get it by a handshake or through a break in the skin. The only ways for it to pass from one person to another are through sexual activity or childbirth.

Gonorrhea in Men

When a healthy man has sex with a partner who has gonorrhea, the bacteria enter the part of the body used during sex—the penis, mouth, or rectum. Gonorrhea is commonly found in the penis. The gonorrhea bacteria enter the urethra through the opening at the head of the penis. The urethra is a tube in the penis. The tube carries the man's sperm and his urine. In the urethra, the bacteria start to multiply. Every 10 to 15 minutes they double in number. Within hours there are millions. This incubation (growing) period can last up to 28 days. The usual incubation period is one to ten days. The body tries to fight the infection. But the white blood cells are quickly outnumbered. The dead white blood cells and the bacteria form pus. The pus collects in the infected area and begins to ooze.

After incubation, the symptoms begin to appear. There is usually a burning feeling when urinating. Pus oozes from the penis. This is when most people realize that something is wrong and go to the doctor or clinic. It is better, however, to treat gonorrhea before these symptoms appear. Otherwise, it can be even more serious.

Bacteria will travel from the urethra to other male sex organs, the testicles. Pus in these organs can leave scar tissue. The scar tissue can cause a man to become sterile. That means he is unable to have children. Untreated gonorrhea can also cause arthritis and heart trouble.

A man is just as likely to have gonorrhea as a woman. And a man can give gonorrhea to a woman during sex. A woman can also give it to a man. When persons are infected, chances are they will infect a partner during sex.

Often, one partner will blame the other for "giving" him or her gonorrhea. This attitude may be unfair. When two people have sex, they are both responsible for what happens. If a person knows, however, that he or she has an STD, it is only fair that he or she tell any sex partners about the STD. STDs are always a serious matter.

Gonorrhea in Women

When a healthy woman has sex with a partner who has gonorrhea, the bacteria enter through the part of the body used during sex. Most often the bacteria enter through the vagina. When they enter through the vagina the bacteria are placed in the cervix. The cervix is the opening of the uterus. It is hidden from sight.

Sometimes the infection will cause a mild burning during urination. Sometimes there will be pus from the vagina. But it is most common for no symptoms to be seen at all.

When the bacteria travel to the other sex organs the infection is more serious. The bacteria will settle in the uterus and/or fallopian tubes. These are important organs for reproduction. When these organs are infected there is pus inside. This pus builds up and causes swelling and pain. There can also be fever and pain in the belly. If gonorrhea is left untreated, the woman may eventually become sterile. That means she will not be able to have children.

A pregnant woman may become infected with gonorrhea. If the disease is not cured, the baby can pick up the bacteria during birth. The pus will get into the baby's eyes. This can cause blindness.

How Is Gonorrhea Treated?

Gonorrhea bacteria can be detected under a microscope. A pus sample will show the bacteria.

In many states, gonorrhea is no longer treated with penicillin. That is because some kinds of bacteria are not killed by penicillin. Patients in these states are treated with other medication that can kill the bacteria.

Gonorrhea is dangerous for a pregnant woman. It can cause blindness in the baby.

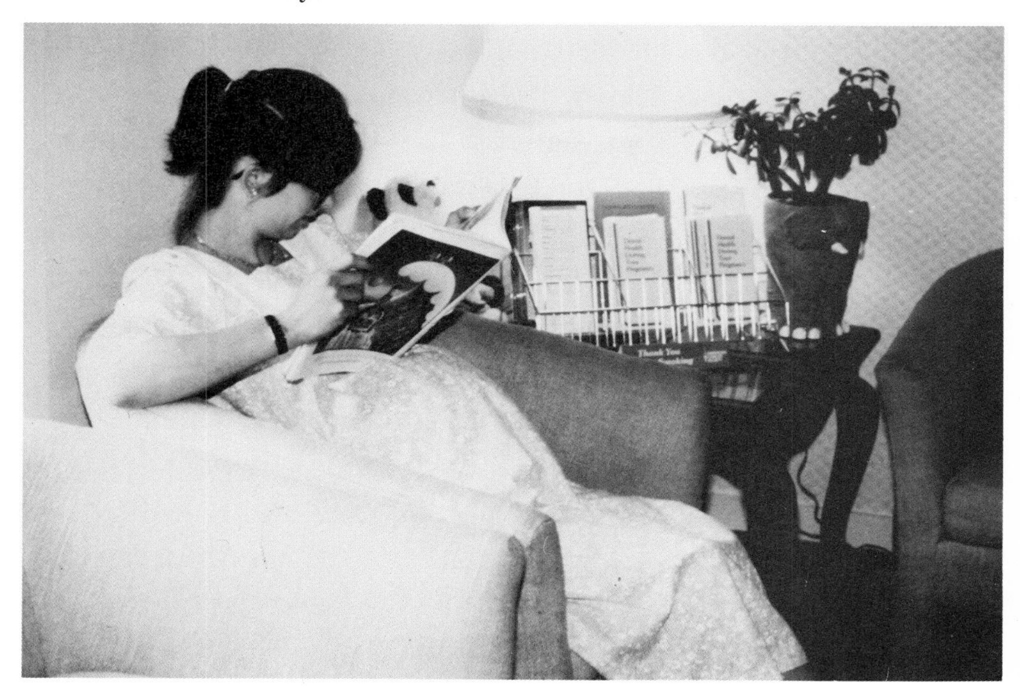

The Chlamydia Epidemic

Many health experts suggest that chlamydia is the fastest-spreading STD in America. Some reports indicate that, in the 1990s, there will be more than 5 million new cases every year. Chlamydia is caused by the bacteria *Chlamydia trachomatis*. It is transmitted by direct contact with the genitals, rectum, or mouth during sex.

Symptoms (signs) of a chlamydia infection may appear within a week of exposure. Sometimes it can take up to a month for symptoms to appear. The symptoms can be very difficult to spot. About 80 percent of women do not have any symptoms that they can see or feel. Many men will not notice symptoms either. The seriousness of chlamydia will only be felt when the infection advances.

The symptoms of chlamydia are like those of gonorrhea. For women, the infection can cause discharge from the vagina. Women may also have a "burning" feeling when urinating. Some women may also have lower pain in their sides, a low-grade fever, and bleeding in between periods. The disease can also affect a woman's ability to have a child. Men may experience burning during urination, discharge from the penis, and a low-grade fever. Burning and itching around the penis may also occur. Sometimes the testicles will swell up.

If chlamydia is not treated it can cause serious health problems. Fortunately, the infection can be treated and cured with antibiotics.

Gonorrhea and Chlamydia: Facts at a Glance

1. Both gonorrhea and chlamydia are widespread STDs. Together they infect millions of Americans each year. Chlamydia is now believed to be the fastest spreading STD in the world.
2. Both diseases are caused by bacteria. These bacteria are transmitted by direct contact with genitals, the mouth, or anus during sex.
3. Left untreated, both diseases can cause serious physical problems, including sterility and harm to newborn babies.
4. Both diseases can usually be prevented by "safer sex," particularly the use of a condom.

Support groups can help people deal with diseases like herpes.

Chapter 6

Genital Herpes: One of Many Herpes

Dear Kim,

Thanks for your letter telling me why you haven't called me. I thought it was something more serious. I thought you had been in an accident or something.

Now I understand why you didn't want to date me anymore. I know you were afraid. But herpes doesn't mean you have to lock yourself away forever. It only means you and your partner have to be careful. A partner can only catch it from you at certain times. And there are precautions we can use to be safer.

I have grown to love you. And I'm not willing to let that go down the drain just because of this. You're right, it is a problem. But it can be dealt with. The most important thing is that you told me. And I understand. And I don't think any less of you because of it. I don't think you're "dirty." I know that has nothing to do with it.

I understand. And I hope you'll answer my next call so I can tell you in person. See you soon.

Cal

There are many different kinds of herpes. All herpes are caused by viruses.

Viruses are too small to be seen with the naked eye. Even a light microscope cannot see them. Some viruses can be seen with a super-powerful microscope called an electron microscope.

Viruses enter the body through the nose, mouth, or skin. Measles, mumps, chicken pox, influenza (the flu), and the common cold are all caused by viruses.

One thing is puzzling about viruses. They do not look or act like living cells. Most cells are "alive." They perform functions such as taking in food, digesting food, and getting rid of waste. They also reproduce. Scientists do not consider viruses to be "alive." That is because they do not take in food or digest food. All they do is reproduce. And they only "come alive" when they are inside another cell.

Not all living cells can be attacked by viruses. The host cell (a cell that a virus lives in) must have a special membrane. The virus needs to attach itself to the membrane. Once the virus is attached, it invades the living cell. The virus uses the cell's materials to reproduce itself. The virus takes over the living cell completely.

The virus reproduces itself many times in the first host cell. Soon the cell bursts open and re-

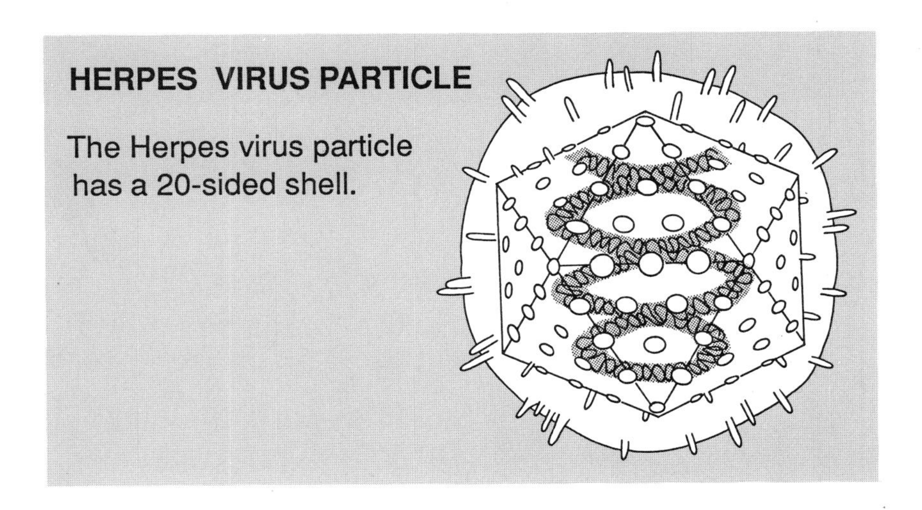

HERPES VIRUS PARTICLE

The Herpes virus particle has a 20-sided shell.

leases virus particles into the body. These viruses invade more cells. And each of those cells then hosts the growth of more virus particles.

The Herpes Virus Group

Herpes in Greek means "to creep." The virus was named this because it can hide in the body for a long time without being detected. Then, without warning, it can come out and cause trouble.

Five Types of Herpes

There are five kinds of herpes virus. Not all herpes viruses are sexually transmitted. One causes chicken pox and "shingles" in adults, another causes mononucleosis ("mono"), and another causes cytomegalovirus (CMV). Herpes simplex 1 (HSV-1) causes cold sores and blisters, usually on the mouth, and Herpes simplex 2 (HSV-2) causes genital herpes.

HSV-1 is transmitted by kissing or touching someone who has a "cold sore" or is "shedding." Shedding means transmitting diseased cells without having a sore or blister. The virus can stay inside the body for a long time. It will usually appear during times of stress and when the body's resistance is low. HSV-1 can sometimes be passed by sexual contact and is often mixed with HSV-2.

HSV-2 is venereal herpes. It is also called genital herpes. It is a sexually transmitted disease (STD). HSV-2 can enter the body through the mucous membranes of the mouth, rectum, penis, or vagina. Herpes sores will then appear at the site of the infection.

The symptoms are usually the worst when a person is initially infected. The person may have a burning and itching at the sores. There may also be numbness (lack of feeling), headache, and fever. Often the person has muscle aches and swollen glands. Usually a person also has poor appetite and a lack of energy.

Herpes symptoms can occur again later. Once the herpes virus is in the body, it does not leave. It is there for life. Herpes is not like gonorrhea or syphilis. There is no known cure for HSV-2. Usually, the symptoms in later outbreaks are not as bad as they are the first time. The later outbreaks can have sores. All outbreaks are uncomfortable.

Herpes causes a great deal of emotional discomfort, too. Many who have it are constantly worried about when symptoms will reappear. They must also worry about giving the disease to others. But genital herpes is usually contagious only at certain times.

Herpes is believed to already have infected more than 20 million people in the United States. Experts believe that between 200,000 to 500,000 new cases are reported each year.

Herpes: Facts at a Glance

1. Herpes is a virus. Viruses cannot be cured.
2. There are five kinds of herpes. Two kinds can be transmitted by sexual contact: HSV-1 and HSV-2. The HSV-1 virus produces cold sores. The HSV-2 virus is genital herpes.
3. Herpes symptoms can be painful. They can include open sores, swelling and pain in the genitals, and achy muscles and joints.
4. Herpes can be treated but not cured.
5. Genital herpes can be prevented. Avoid sex with someone who is shedding or has open sores. Use condoms to reduce the chances of infection.

Responsible sex involves open discussion and honesty with your sexual partner.

Chapter 7

Genital Warts

Genital warts are also called venereal warts. They are fast becoming one of the most common STDs in the United States. About 1 million people get genital warts each year.

Venereal warts are growths that appear on the parts of the body that are used during sex. They include the penis, the vagina, the anus, and the back of the throat. The warts are caused by viruses. And the viruses spread only through sexual contact.

Often, the warts look harmless. But they should be treated as soon as possible. They can multiply and spread very quickly. And the longer they grow, the harder it is to get rid of them.

The viruses that cause warts are spread during sex. Warts might appear a few weeks after exposure. Or they might take months to appear. But just because you cannot see the warts does not mean they are not there. A person can be infected and pass the virus on without knowing it.

The warts usually look like tiny cauliflowers. They are bumpy. But sometimes they are flat. Some warts are so small that they can only be seen under a microscope. They can sometimes cause itching. But they do not usually cause pain.

The best way to make sure you do not have genital warts is to see a doctor. Have her or him check any strange growths, sores, or skin changes you may have. Sores or growths near or on your penis, vagina, or anus are very important. If you do have warts, the doctor can remove them. Small warts can be treated with a liquid that dissolves them. Larger warts can be removed by freezing them. These methods are not expensive. They do not hurt, and removal is usually done in the doctor's office.

If you find out that you have genital warts, tell your sex partner(s). They may have the virus too.

Genital Warts: Facts at a Glance

1. Genital warts are a very common STD in the United States. They are growths that appear on the parts of the body used during sex.
2. Warts should be treated as soon as possible.

Conclusion

There are other sexually transmitted diseases. Many can be just as serious as those we have discussed. But those diseases are less common than the ones we have learned about.

Some sexually transmitted problems are not as serious as herpes, or gonorrhea, or syphilis. But they are still problems. Pubic lice can be shared during sexual or close contact. And so can scabies. Scabies are tiny "mite-like" creatures that live on the skin. The symptoms of these two problems are similar. Usually they cause rashes and itching. They can be treated with a medicated shampoo, powder, or lotion.

Teenagers can get information or advice from parents or counselors.

The Teen and Sex: Special Problems

Teens have an especially hard time with their feelings about sex. Puberty and adolescence are very confusing times. Teens have sexual urges that they have never had before. Sometimes teens ignore the fact that sex requires some precaution.

Most teens experience emotional changes during puberty. New sexual desires make teens feel anxious. Teens may think that changes in their bodies are scary and embarrassing. The thought of sex can be both exciting and scary . Often teens find it hard to handle the responsibilities of sexual activity. They make excuses. They say it is too hard for them to think about "safer sex" when sex itself is so new to them.

The most important thing for teens to remember is *responsibility.* That means being grown-up about what you do. It means remembering that what you do today can affect what happens tomorrow. It means thinking about the risks of sex. And making decisions.

What we have learned in this book can make all teens more responsible. Let's review some of the most important facts:

1. It is most important to take good care of yourself. That means paying attention to your body. And seeing a doctor or nurse if it is needed.
2. Some STDs can be cured.
3. Some STDs cannot be cured.
4. It is always best to treat STDs as early as possible.
5. The risk of getting an STD is greatly reduced by "safer sex." That means using condoms.
6. You can reduce risks by knowing some background about your sexual partners. Reducing the number of partners you have will also reduce risks.

This book has shown you how serious STDs are. It has told you how important it is to prevent them, and that prevention is not very difficult.

Maybe you have even thought about things you can do to be more careful about sex. And you can probably see that a little prevention can save you a great deal of trouble later.

Glossary—*Explaining New Words*

acute stage Very serious stage.

AIDS Acquired immunodeficiency syndrome, a sexually transmitted virus.

antibodies Organisms made by the immune system that fight infection and disease in the body.

cervix Inside vagina, the opening of the uterus.

communicable Contagious, passed from one person to another.

condom Contraceptive, a rubber casing that is placed over the erect penis.

contagious Transmitted from one person to another.

cytomegalovirus Herpes virus passed to newborn babies by the mother.

embryo Fertilized egg in early stages of development.

fallopian tubes Tubes that carry eggs from the ovaries to the uterus.

fatigue Tiredness.

fertilize To start life.

fetus Fertilized egg in later stages of development.
fungus Tiny plant growths that grow on the body.
genital herpes Sexually transmitted virus.
gonorrhea Sexually transmitted bacteria.
homosexual "Gay," person who has sex with another of the same sex.
immune system Fights infection in the body.
incubation Growth time.
infectious Contagious, able to be passed from one person to another.
latent Hidden.
menstruation "Period," monthly female bleeding.
mucous membrane Soft lining inside organs like mouth, vagina, and rectum.
ovaries Organs that contain the eggs in a female.
paralysis Inability to move.
pelvis Lower abdominal area, near the genitals.
penis Male external sex organ.
puberty The beginning of sexual feelings and growth of sexual organs.
pus White liquid that collects in sores and infected areas.
rectum Anus.
"safer sex" Sex with condoms to prevent transmitting STDs.
scrotum Sac that holds the testes (testicles).
semen Liquid from penis containing sperm.
shedding Transmitting disease cells without having a sore or blister.
sperm Male fertilizing organisms.

spirochete Germ that causes syphilis.
STDs Sexually transmitted diseases.
syphilis A sexually transmitted disease.
testicles Testes, produce sperm in the male.
transfusion (blood) Putting one person's blood into another person.
tumors Bumps or lumps of tissues that form in the body.
urethra Tube that carries male's sperm and urine through penis.
uterus Womb, sac in which the fetus develops.
vagina Female opening to sexual organs.
VD Venereal disease, sexually transmitted diseases.
virus Organism that invades the cells of the body.

Where to Get Help

AIDS Action Council
Federation of AIDS-Related Organizations
729 Eighth Street SE
Washington, DC 20003
(202) 547-3101

Herpes Resource Center
P.O. Box 100
Palo Alto, CA 94302
(415) 328-7710

American Foundation for the Prevention of Venereal Disease
799 Broadway
New York, NY 10003
(212) 759-2069

Birth Control Institute
1242 Lincoln Avenue
Anaheim, CA 92805
(714) 956-4630

Public Health Service, Centers for Disease Control
U.S. Public Health Service
1600 Clifton Road NE
Atlanta, GA 30333
(404) 329-3534
Hotline: 1-800-442-366

National Coalition of Gay Sexually Transmitted Disease Services
P.O. Box 239
Milwaukee, WI 53201
(414) 277-7671

For Further Reading

Barlow, David. *Sexually Transmitted Diseases: The Facts.* New York: Oxford University Press, 1979. A study of the causes, symptoms, and cures for STDs.

Connell, Elizabeth B., and Tatum, Howard J. *Sexually Transmitted Diseases: Diagnosis and Treatment.* New York: Creative Infomatics, 1985. How to identify symptoms and treat STDs safely and effectively.

Edwards, Gabrielle. *Coping with Venereal Disease,* rev. ed. New York: Rosen Publishing Group, 1988. Covers human reproductive systems, the history of each disease, statistics, and contains a question-and-answer section.

Ulene, Art. *Safe Sex in a Dangerous World.* New York: Vintage Books, 1987. Prevention methods for STDs with discussions about responsibility and other sexual behaviors.

Zinner, Stephen. *How to Protect Yourself from STDs.* New York: Summit Books, 1986. A handbook of prevention methods, as well as a discussion of treatments.

Index

About the Author
Samuel G. Woods is a New York-based writer who specializes in writing for young adults. He currently works in Manhattan, where he also does freelance editing and photography.

About the Editor
Evan Stark is a well-known sociologist, educator, and therapist as well as a popular lecturer on women's and children's health issues. Dr. Stark was the Henry Rutgers Fellow at Rutgers University, an associate at the Institute for Social and Policy Studies at Yale University, and a Fulbright Fellow at the University of Essex. He is the author of many publications in the field of family relations and is the father of four children.

Acknowledgments and Photo Credits
Cover: Charles Waldon. All other photos by Stuart Rabinowitz:; pp. 7, 22, 49, Sonja Kalter.

Design/Production: Blackbirch Graphics, Inc.